Lerner SPORTS

WOMEN GOT GAME

WOMEN'S PROFESSIONAL TENNIS

MARGARET J. GOLDSTEIN

Lerner Publications ◆ Minneapolis

Copyright © 2026 by Lerner Publishing Group, Inc.

All rights reserved. International copyright secured. No part of this book may be reproduced, stored in a retrieval system, or transmitted in any form or by any means—electronic, mechanical, photocopying, recording, or otherwise—without the prior written permission of Lerner Publishing Group, Inc., except for the inclusion of brief quotations in an acknowledged review.

Lerner Publications Company
An imprint of Lerner Publishing Group, Inc.
241 First Avenue North
Minneapolis, MN 55401 USA

For reading levels and more information, look up this title at www.lernerbooks.com.

Main body text set in Aptifer Slab LT Pro.
Typeface provided by Linotype AG.

Editor: Brianna Kaiser **Designer:** Mary Ross
Lerner team: Sue Marquis

Library of Congress Cataloging-in-Publication Data

Names: Goldstein, Margaret J., author.
Title: Women's professional tennis / Margaret J. Goldstein.
Description: Minneapolis : Lerner Publications , 2026. | Series: Lerner sports. Women got game | Includes bibliographical references and index. | Audience: Ages 7–11 | Audience: Grades 2–3 | Summary: "Women from all around the world compete in the Women's Tennis Association. From Billie Jean King to Serena Williams and Coco Gauff, learn about the past and present WTA stars and the league's biggest moments"— Provided by publisher.
Identifiers: LCCN 2024042724 (print) | LCCN 2024042725 (ebook) | ISBN 9798765668917 (library binding) | ISBN 9798765683644 (paperback) | ISBN 9798765682418 (epub)
Subjects: LCSH: Women tennis players—Biography—Juvenile literature. | Women's Tennis Association—Juvenile literature.
Classification: LCC GV994.A1 R54 2026 (print) | LCC GV994.A1 (ebook) | DDC 796.3420092/52—dc23/eng/20241208

LC record available at https://lccn.loc.gov/2024042724
LC ebook record available at https://lccn.loc.gov/2024042725

Manufactured in the United States of America
1-1011987-53862-2/6/2025

TABLE OF CONTENTS

TENNIS TRIUMPH 4
FAST FACTS 5

CHAPTER 1
EQUAL MEASURES 8

CHAPTER 2
GREAT WTA MOMENTS 13

CHAPTER 3
BEST OF THE BEST 22

GLOSSARY. 30
LEARN MORE. 31
INDEX. 32

TENNIS TRIUMPH

Coco Gauff wanted a trophy. The 19-year-old rising star had reached the final of the 2023 US Open, one of the four major tennis tournaments. If she won the final, she'd have her first major title.

The match wouldn't be easy. Gauff's opponent, Aryna Sabalenka, had won the Australian Open earlier that year. And she was ranked number 2 in the world.

Sabalenka played like a champion in the first set. She beat Gauff six games to two. But Gauff came back strong and won the second set 6–3.

With a 5–2 lead in the third set, Gauff stayed focused. She served for the title. *Bam!* Her serve rocketed across the net. The two women drilled the ball back and forth. Then Sabalenka knocked a backhand into the front court.

FAST FACTS

- FOUNDED IN 1877, WIMBLEDON IS THE OLDEST MAJOR TENNIS TOURNAMENT.
- SERENA WILLIAMS HOLDS THE WOMEN'S OPEN ERA RECORD FOR THE MOST MAJOR SINGLES TITLES.
- COCO GAUFF HAS WON MAJOR TITLES IN BOTH SINGLES AND DOUBLES PLAY.
- IN 2022, ONS JABEUR BECAME THE FIRST ARAB AND AFRICAN WOMAN IN THE OPEN ERA TO REACH A MAJOR FINAL.

Gauff raced forward and reached to return it. Her return shot flew past Sabalenka.

The crowd erupted in cheers. With that point, Gauff had her victory. She was the US Open champion.

Gauff, Sabalenka, and other top female tennis players are part of the Women's Tennis Association (WTA). The WTA Tour includes the majors and other tournaments. The WTA also promotes women's tennis around the world. With the support of the WTA, many female players have become rich and famous.

Coco Gauff serving in the 2023 US Open final

Gauff celebrates winning the US Open in 2023.

Chapter 1
EQUAL MEASURES

Suzanne Lenglen competes in the 1920 French Open.

Tennis is hundreds of years old. In the late 1800s, players began to form tennis clubs and tournaments. Over time, they started the four major tournaments: Wimbledon (in England) in 1877, the US Open in 1881, the French Open in 1891, and the Australian Open in 1905.

Some players turned pro. Tour organizers paid them to play matches. But only amateurs could compete in the majors. The rules changed in 1968. That year, pros could play in the majors for the first time.

At Wimbledon in 1968, Billie Jean King won the women's singles title. She earned 750 British pounds in prize money. Rod Laver won the men's singles title. His prize was 2,000 pounds, more than twice King's award.

Billie Jean King playing in Wimbledon on July 5, 1968

King and eight other female players called this unfair. They wanted more money for female players. They founded a women's tour in 1971. King and the other women founded the WTA in 1973. The WTA made deals with TV stations to show matches. It signed on big companies as sponsors.

BATTLE OF THE SEXES

In 1973, former tennis pro Bobby Riggs said he was better than any female pro. Billie Jean King agreed to play him. In a match called the Battle of the Sexes, she beat Riggs 6–4, 6–3, 6–3.

Chris Evert hits a backhand during the 1985 French Open final.

The WTA also pushed tournaments to pay higher prize money to women. At the 1973 US Open, the male and female winners of the singles titles got the same prize money: $25,000. But other tournaments still paid men more than women.

In the late 1970s, women's tennis soared in popularity. Fans packed into stadiums and tuned in on TV to see star players such as Chris Evert and Evonne Goolagong Cawley. Prize money amounts got bigger and bigger.

After more than 50 years, the WTA is still going strong. By 2024, more than 1,650 players from 85 countries were part of the WTA. The WTA Tour includes more than 50 tournaments per year, plus the four majors.

SINGLES AND DOUBLES

Evonne Goolagong Cawley, a member of the Wiradjuri people, was the first female Australian Aboriginal sports star. She learned to play tennis with a homemade racket. Coaches saw her talent and helped her enter tournaments. Between 1971 and 1980, she won seven major singles titles and six major doubles titles.

Evonne Goolagong Cawley serving in 1976

Chapter 2

GREAT WTA MOMENTS

Steffi Graf competing in the 1987 French Open

The WTA story is packed with amazing moments. At the 1987 French Open, Steffi Graf was on a mission. The 17-year-old wanted her first major win, but she'd have to beat Martina Navratilova, ranked number 1 in the world.

The two women battled on the dusty clay court. They each won a set. The third was long and hard. At one point, it looked like the end for Graf. Navratilova was up 5–3 and needed just one more game to triumph, but then she started making mistakes. Graf dug in, evened the score, and then pulled ahead to take the set 8–6. After this first major win, Graf dominated women's tennis for a decade.

Martina Navratilova plays a forehand return against Graf in the 1987 French Open.

Jennifer Capriati playing in the 2002 Australian Open final

The year was 2002. Things looked bleak for Jennifer Capriati at the Australian Open. The powerful Martina Hingis had won the first set. She led in the second set four games to none. Hingis served for match point, which would win the game, set, and match. But Capriati scored instead.

DOUBLE FEATURE

Although many top players only focus on singles, some players, such as Coco Gauff, play both doubles and singles. In 2024, Gauff and her playing partner, Kateřina Siniaková, won the French Open doubles title.

Gauff celebrates with her doubles partner, Kateřina Siniaková (*right*), after winning the 2024 French Open.

Hingis served for another match point. Again, Capriati made the score. Capriati saved herself from defeat a third time and then a fourth before winning the set. Hingis was rattled. Capriati had newfound confidence. She easily won the third set to take the title. Her Australian Open victory was one of the greatest come-from-behind wins in tennis history.

Serena Williams stood across the net from her older sister Venus. The two were finalists at the 2017 Australian Open. After winning the first set and leading 5–4 in the third, Serena served for the match point. The ball zoomed across the net. Venus returned it just as hard. After a short rally, Venus struggled to make a shot. She hit the ball out of bounds.

Serena Williams serves at the Australian Open in 2017.

Williams wins the 2017 Australian Open.

Serena raised her arms in triumph. This victory was extra special. It was Serena's 23rd major singles title, a new record for the Open Era of women's tennis. Williams was already called the best woman ever to play the game. This record only added to her greatness.

At the 2018 US Open, everyone expected Williams to win her 24th major title. Her opponent was 20-year-old Naomi Osaka. Osaka had been quickly moving up the WTA ranks. She was excited to play against Williams, one of her childhood idols. With her powerful serve and strong forehand, Osaka shocked the crowd. She outplayed the 36-year-old champion to win the match in two sets. It was a stunning upset.

Naomi Osaka serves at the 2018 US Open.

In 2021, few people knew the name Emma Raducanu. The teen hadn't played in many WTA tournaments. She entered the US Open as a qualifier. This meant she had to win three early matches before she could compete in the main event. She won them all and kept on winning.

Emma Raducanu plays a forehand return during the final match of the 2021 US Open.

Raducanu holding her trophy after winning the 2021 US Open

Raducanu made it all the way to the finals, where she beat Leylah Fernandez in two sets. In the history of the Open Era, no qualifier had ever won a major title. Raducanu's WTA ranking jumped from 150 to 23. She became a star overnight.

Chapter 3

BEST OF THE BEST

Graf plays a backhand return in the 1989 French Open final.

The history of the WTA is filled with star power. Steffi Graf won 22 major singles titles, holding the record until Serena Williams passed her in 2017. Graff also achieved a Golden Slam—winning all four majors and an Olympic gold medal. She was ranked number 1 in the world for 186 weeks in a row and 377 weeks total.

Monica Seles was one of the most powerful hitters in women's tennis. Her serves sped over the net as fast as 105 miles (169 km) per hour. In the 1990s, Seles won the French Open three times, the Australian Open four times, and the US Open twice.

Monica Seles playing in the final at Wimbledon in 1992

WINNING WAYS

In 1984, Martina Navratilova won 74 matches straight. That's the longest winning streak in the history of women's tennis. Navratilova finished her career with an impressive tally of titles: three at the Australian Open, two at the French Open, four at the US Open, and nine at Wimbledon.

Venus Williams turned pro when she was 14, in 1994. She played older, more experienced women and showed she could win matches. In 2000, she won her first Wimbledon title and her first US Open. She won the US Open again in 2001, this time defeating her sister Serena. By 2002, she was number 1 in the world. She added four more Wimbledon championships by the end of the decade.

Serena Williams arrived on the WTA tour a year after her sister. She started beating top 10 players and won her first major, the US Open, in 1999. From then on, she was the queen of the WTA. She entered the record books with 23 major titles. She is the only tennis player to have Golden Slams in both singles and doubles.

Serena Williams hits a backhand during the 2007 Australian Open final.

Serena Williams was the biggest name in women's tennis for two decades, but she wasn't the only star then. Her rivals in the first two decades of the 2000s included Angelique Kerber, Maria Sharapova, and Caroline Wozniacki. All three won big WTA tournaments, including majors, and all three held the number 1 ranking for a time.

WINNING SISTERS

The Williams sisters teamed up for years to play doubles tennis. Together, Venus and Serena played at 14 major doubles championships. They won all 14. They also won the gold medal for doubles at the 2000, 2008, and 2012 Olympic Games.

Iga Świątek competing in the 2024 French Open

New WTA players challenge the more experienced champions. After defeating Serena Williams at the 2018 US Open, Naomi Osaka won the Open again in 2020. She also won the Australian Open in 2019 and 2021.

Iga Świątek also became a superstar. With one of the most powerful forehands in the WTA, she won the French Open in 2020, 2022, 2023, and 2024. She also won the US Open in 2022.

Ons Jabeur celebrates winning the quarterfinal match of the 2022 US Open.

Ons Jabeur had a slow and steady rise through the WTA ranks, eventually reaching number 2. She joined the tour in 2012. For many years, she played well, but she never got much attention. That changed in 2022, when she made it to two major finals: Wimbledon and the US Open. She lost both matches, but she gained fame.

Jabeur comes from Tunisia, a nation in North Africa. She was the first Arab and African woman in the Open Era to reach a major tennis final. She has won five singles WTA tournaments.

Women's tennis is more popular than ever. The sport will keep growing, and young players will continue to challenge the experienced superstars. They will bring new energy to the WTA.

Jabeur makes a return during the 2022 US Open.

GLOSSARY

Aboriginal: a person whose ancestors were among the earliest human inhabitants of Australia

amateur: playing a sport without being paid

backhand: a tennis stroke made with the back of the hand turned in the direction in which the hand is moving

game: a part of a set that is won when a player wins at least four points

major: also known as Grand Slam, one of the four biggest tennis tournaments: the Australian Open, the French Open, the US Open, and Wimbledon (in England)

Open Era: the modern era of pro tennis, which began in 1968

pro: short for *professional*, taking part in an activity to make money

qualifier: a person who must win extra early rounds of a tournament before being allowed to compete in the main rounds

rally: a series of hits back and forth over the net

set: in tennis, a group of six or more games

sponsor: a business that pays some of the costs of something in exchange for advertisement of its products

LEARN MORE

Fabiny, Sarah. *Who Is Billie Jean King?* New York: Penguin Workshop, 2024.

Kiddle: Billie Jean King Facts for Kids
https://kids.kiddle.co/Billie_Jean_King

Leed, Percy. *Meet Naomi Osaka: Tennis Superstar*. Minneapolis: Lerner Publications, 2025.

Ridge, Yolanda. *Coco Gauff vs. Serena Williams: Who Would Win?* Minneapolis: Lerner Publications, 2025.

Time for Kids: The Greatest
https://www.timeforkids.com/g34/the-greatest-g3/?rl=en-700

WTA: About the WTA
https://www.wtatennis.com/about

INDEX

Australian Open, 5, 8, 15–17, 23–24, 27

Battle of the Sexes, 10

doubles, 5, 12, 16, 25–26

French Open, 8, 13, 16, 23–24, 27

Golden Slam, 22, 25

match point, 15–17

Open Era, 5, 18, 21, 29

prize money, 9, 11

ranking, 5, 13, 19, 21–22, 26, 28

serve, 5, 15–17, 19

US Open, 4–6, 8, 11, 19–20, 23–25, 27–28

Wimbledon, 5, 8–9, 24, 28
winning streak, 24

PHOTO ACKNOWLEDGMENTS

Image credits: Tim Clayton/Corbis via Getty Images, pp. 4, 19; Frey/TPN/Getty Images, p. 6; Sarah Stier/Getty Images, p. 7; Underwood Archives/Alamy, p. 8; Mirrorpix/Getty Images, p. 9; Trevor Jones/Allsport/Getty Images, p. 11; Don Morley/Allsport/Getty Images, p. 12; Leo Mason/Popperfoto via Getty Images, p. 13; Chris Cole/Allsport/Getty Images, p. 14; Professional Sport/Popperfoto via Getty Images/Getty Images, p. 15; Dan Istitene/Getty Images, p. 16; Cameron Spencer/Getty Images, p. 17; Greg Wood/AFP via Getty Images, p. 18; Matthew Stockman/Getty Images, p. 20; J. Conrad Williams. Jr./Newsday RM via Getty Images, p. 21; Simon Bruty/Allsport/Getty Images, p. 22; Chris Smith/Popperfoto via Getty Images/Getty Images, p. 23; Clive Brunskill/Getty Images, pp. 25, 27; Jamie Squire/Getty Images, p. 28; Julian Finney/Getty Images, p. 29.

Cover images: Garrett Ellwood/USTA via AP (top); Corinne Dubreuil/Abaca/Sipa USA via AP (bottom).